To

_____

From

_____

Stress *Less*

and Enjoy Each Day

DAVID ZERFOSS

THOMAS NELSON
Since 1798

NASHVILLE   DALLAS   MEXICO CITY   RIO DE JANEIRO   BEIJING

Stress Less and Enjoy Each Day

© 2012 Simple Truths

Published in Nashville, Tennessee, by Thomas Nelson. Thomas Nelson is a registered trademark of Thomas Nelson, Inc.

Originally published by Simple Truths LLC
1952 McDowell Road, Suite 300
Naperville, IL 60563
Toll Free: 800.900.3427
www.simpletruths.com

This edition published under license from Simple Truths exclusively for Thomas Nelson, Inc.

Thomas Nelson, Inc., titles may be purchased in bulk for educational, business, fund-raising, or sales promotional use. For information, please e-mail SpecialMarkets@ThomasNelson.com.

Unless otherwise noted, Scripture quotations are taken from THE NEW KING JAMES VERSION. © 1982 by Thomas Nelson, Inc. Used by permission. All rights reserved.

Scripture quotations marked NLT are from the *Holy Bible*, New Living Translation. © 1996. Used by permission of Tyndale House Publishers, Inc., Wheaton, Illinois 60189. All rights reserved.

Scripture quotations marked MSG are from *The Message* by Eugene H. Peterson. © 1993, 1994, 1995, 1996, 2000. Used by permission of NavPress Publishing Group. All rights reserved.

Scripture quotations marked NIV are taken from the Holy Bible, New International Version®, NIV®. Copyright © 1973, 1978, 1984 by Biblica, Inc™. Used by permission of Zondervan. All rights reserved worldwide. www.zondervan.com

ISBN: 978-1-4003-2031-8

Printed in Singapore

12 13 14 15 16 TWP 6 5 4 3 2 1

Table of Contents

FOREWORD *by Joe Gibbs*

*The **great reason** why*

life is troubled and restless

lies not without, but within.

—ALEXANDER MACLAREN

I've been known to run my life at a pretty fast pace. Whether it's been the pursuit of coaching an NFL team to a Super Bowl championship or pushing the limits in capturing a NASCAR Cup Series championship, like many of you, the busy-ness of my daily activities and expectations of "doing more" have in the past created choices that led to more or less stress in my life.

Oftentimes, our daily schedules control us, rather than us having the ability to control what had we set out to do. However, *we* make the choice to continue adding to our to-do list even when it doesn't make sense. The reality is this: there is all the time in the world if we just learn to prioritize our to-dos in light of what we can actually get done.

I know you're probably thinking, *But my job has expectations that I must meet!* or, *My family runs at 110 miles per hour— I can't just stop!* Whatever your stress is, author and friend David Zerfoss can reveal how to choose less stress in your everyday life. And David's ten principles will show you a different way of approaching life that will reduce your stress without affecting your productivity.

If you feel like your stress level is off the charts, *Stress Less and Enjoy Each Day* will provide you with a new perspective that can and will change your life. It's like having an inspired road map to simplifying your life . . . and to choosing less stress. And who wouldn't want that?

Remember, it's about choices—important decisions that will help free your life of the unwanted and, frankly, unneeded stress that tends to control our emotions and our actions.

Live with intention and without the stress,

Joe Gibbs

INTRODUCTION

"**Do not worry** *about tomorrow.*"

—MATTHEW 6:34

everal years ago, during my pastor's Sunday sermon, he spoke about how life is made up of a series of choices. It made me realize that my hectic professional and personal life was of my choosing.

I had *chosen to live like this.*

Many of us hurry through life going from one place to the next—focused on conquering the next mountain, making the next deal, running the next errand—believing we will never have enough time to do all the things we need to get done. Yet there is all the time in the world if we just realize that life is a series of choices and that being free from stress is one of those choices. Jesus enters and He says to us, "Do not worry about tomorrow" (Matthew 6:34), and we think to ourselves, *Really? Is that even possible? That's how I live!*

Whether it's your business life that is overly complicated or your personal life (or both!), you have chosen this current system of chaos. What Jesus called "the cares of this world" (Mark 4:19) are a tantalizing swirl of getting the next "fix," tempting us to fit more and more things, people, and processes into our lives, personally and professionally. And because we are so busy being busy, it's easy to be lured into the fray with our lengthy to-do lists. Yet the greatest achievements often come from the simplest ideas and in the simplest forms.

To experience a simplified life, we first have to learn to slow down long enough to see through all the clutter. We need to realize that we are the powerful magnets that attracted this life to ourselves—no matter what, good or bad.

My wish for you is that after you've read through the ten

principles, you'll commit to simplifying your life and enlist others for support. Take out a blank sheet of paper and prayerfully create the life you truly want to live: a life with less stress and complexity, anchored by the simple words of Jesus and driven by a clear sense of your unique and simple purpose.

Yours for Success,

David R. Taylor

Principle #1

Spot
That
Sprout

ENJOY THE LITTLE THINGS,
for one day
YOU MAY LOOK BACK
and realize they were
THE BIG THINGS.
—ROBERT BRAULT

MANY OF US SEEM TO HAVE *an endless to-do list. But does all that rushing around stop us from seeing the big picture? Taking a moment to step back from our day-to-day schedules can help us simplify our lives—and may even help us identify what we are missing that would keep us energized and fulfilled.*

Mary was *not*
PRAISED FOR SITTING STILL,
but for her
SITTING AT JESUS' FEET.
—CHARLES SPURGEON

Mary kept up a constant and hectic schedule of work travel. It kept her metabolism and adrenaline high. Add this to the fact that she was keeping up with two very active, triple sports–playing teenage sons, which meant there wasn't much time leftover to think about "simplifying." Besides, simple lives were what other people wanted. She was very content. She was busy being busy.

During one business trip out west, Mary traveled with one of her company's sales representatives. His name was Bob, and he was quite up in years. Mary often wondered why Bob continued to work at such an advanced age and chose to keep such a size-able multistate territory.

On this particular trip they were traveling on an especially long car route, visiting customers throughout New Mexico and then on to Colorado. After driving several hours through sparsely populated, very dry, and rocky terrain without even a single traffic light in sight for miles, Bob looked over at Mary and said, "Are you overwhelmed by the vastness of the landscape and wondering when will it ever end?"

"Yes," she replied. "How did you know what I was thinking?"

Bob explained that throughout his many years of traveling this route, everyone who accompanied him felt the very same thing. Then Bob went on to share a profound rule with Mary about simplifying.

Bob explained to Mary that we can all choose to

> Look for what's *missing.* Many advisors can tell a president how to *improve* what's *proposed* or what's gone amiss. Few are able to see what *isn't there.*
>
> —DONALD RUMSFELD

We marvel at the Creator, not only as the one who made heaven and earth . . . but also as the one who made the small creatures. . . . And as in all creation we revere his skill, so the one whose mind is given to Christ is earnest in small things as in great.

—SAINT JEROME

easily get lost in and feel overwhelmed by our surroundings. "Do you see that little tree sprouting up there ahead, among all those large rock formations?" Bob asked. Mary strained her eyes but could not find what he was seeing. As they got closer, Bob pointed out the small sprouting tree he had seen when it was far off in the distance.

Bob shared with Mary that he handled these long drives through hundreds of miles of vast terrain by looking for the little

EVERYONE *is trying to accomplish*
SOMETHING BIG,
not realizing that **LIFE IS MADE UP OF**
LITTLE THINGS.
—FRANK HOWARD CLARK

things amid the overwhelming, complex landscape. He didn't focus on just seeing what was all around him, but rather he *chose* to look for what he might have been *missing*.

He continued on his drive, merrily searching for and pointing out more little things hiding along the way.

As you go about your day, are you letting yourself become overwhelmed by the vast amount of things in the landscape of your life? Choose to live by one of Bob's rules, and spot that sprout you might otherwise be missing. In the midst of daunting, wide-open spaces, take the time to "be still, and know" that He is God (Psalm 46:10). Did you know that "the whole earth is full of His glory" (Isaiah 6:3)? We need only take the time to look.

SOME QUESTIONS TO ASK YOURSELF:

- What's missing in your life?
- Are you spending too much time on things that don't really matter?
- What's the "sprout" you need to focus on?

Principle #2

Focus on
Priorities

I learned that we can do ANYTHING, *but we can't do* EVERYTHING . . . *at least not at the same time.*

—DAN MILLMAN

LIFE CAN BECOME VERY FULL VERY FAST. *If we first block off time for who and what is most important in our lives, it can actually free us up to really focus on all the rest.*

"Seek the Kingdom of God **ABOVE ALL ELSE,** *and live righteously, and he will give you* **EVERYTHING YOU NEED."**
—MATTHEW 6:33 NLT

I've had the pleasure of getting to know Joe Gibbs, three-time Super Bowl championship coach and three-time NASCAR championship team owner. You could say that Joe leads a very active life—one full of things to do and people to see, whether he's on the racetrack or on the football field.

One day I got a glimpse into one of the rules Joe lives by. It's something he commits to only after time spent in a personal relationship with God, through prayer and reading his Bible.

And that's his family time. I'll refer to it as "Pat's time."

As with all busy executives or famous people, in order to get on Joe's schedule, you have to go through his personal assistant, and you have to want him on a date not already marked out as "Pat's time."

What's "Pat's time"? Pat is Joe's wife. As I mentioned earlier, first is Joe's time with God, second comes his time with family. Everything else comes after those first two. Many people may know Joe as a religious man. Well, I can tell you, he's also religious about Pat's time. It's as simple as that. If you want him for something, at best you will be third in line.

You've got to respect a man who lives by simple rules and is so

The first thing FOR OUR SOUL'S HEALTH,
the first thing FOR HIS GLORY,
and the first thing FOR OUR OWN USEFULNESS,

is to keep ourselves in PERPETUAL COMMUNION
with the LORD JESUS.

—CHARLES SPURGEON

*No matter what you've
done for yourself or
for humanity,
if you can't look back
on having given love
and attention to your
own family,* **what have
you really accomplished?**

—ELBERT HUBBARD

The key is not to prioritize what's on your schedule, but to **schedule your priorities.**

—STEPHEN COVEY

true to his convictions. No matter how busy life gets for this world-renowned coach and leader, he has his priorities straight. He chooses to set aside time for what's truly important in his life and in a particular order he feels is most appropriate.

Do you have an order for the priorities in your life, or is everything in competition with each other? Are you so caught up in what's next that you have forgotten the person next to you?

Choose to carve out some "Pat's time" in your life (whatever this may mean for you). You may find that it's *simply* the best time of your life.

SOME QUESTIONS TO ASK YOURSELF:

- Do you have a sequence for your competing priorities?

- Is there time for God in your life?

- Who's your "Pat"?

- Is she or he on your calendar before all the to-dos?

Principle #3

Reduce the
Numbers

It is *not good* to
HAVE EVERYTHING
one *wants.*

—BLAISE PASCAL

IN THIS WORLD OF INSTANT GRATIFICATION *and unlimited choices, we often find ourselves surrounded by mountains of things—furniture, knickknacks, toys (for children and adults), tools, clothes, and so on. Are all these things bringing us real joy and happiness or are they prohibiting us from seeing what really matters? It's amazing what simple rules we can relearn when we open our eyes.*

There are two wings that raise a man ABOVE EARTHLY THINGS, *simplicity and purity.*

—THOMAS À KEMPIS

With the pace of the world today, we are often moving so fast that we don't pause to consider what we really need. Are all these things in our lives adding value or just adding clutter to both our surroundings and our lives? Are they complementing our lives or complicating them? With each additional thing often comes additional stress—how to use it, where to put it, and ultimately how to pay for it.

Looking back on your early childhood, what intrigued and interested you? For many of us, it was the joy of spending time outdoors. One day I had the pleasure of visiting the Niederman family farm in Hamilton, Ohio. The Niedermans have been in farming for many generations. Farming life is so important to them that they open up their home, their land, and their barns so folks can come experience what farm life is like. Among other events at the farm, each October they create a giant corn maze for children and adults to wander through day or night by flashlight.

This past year they were digging out an area for a new addition to their corn maze attraction. A large pile of dirt was placed off to the side until they could determine how to make good use of it somewhere else on the farm. However, they found themselves at the opening day of the corn maze before they got an

> *"If God gives such attention to the appearance of wildflowers—* most of which are never even seen— don't you think *he'll attend to you, take pride in you, do his best for you?"*
>
> —MATTHEW 6:30 MSG

*It is good and fitting for one to eat and drink,
and to enjoy the good of all his labor in which
he toils under the sun all the days of his life
which God gives him; for it is his heritage.*

—KING SOLOMON, ECCLESIASTES 5:18

opportunity to take care of that pile of dirt. Not only was the corn maze a hit as usual, but to their surprise, children immediately gravitated to that large dirt pile. Kids were running up and sliding down this unintentional playing field. There were no blinking lights, no electronics, no sound effects. The sounds of laughter and fun filled the autumn air as kids did what kids do best—be imaginative and seize the moment.

As adults, we often find ourselves acquiring more and more

Eliminate physical clutter.
More importantly,
eliminate spiritual clutter.

—TERRI GUILLEMETS

things for ourselves and our children—whether it's the next great video game, cell phone, computer, or the latest hot new toy. As we add more material things to our lives, we often forget not only what's most important but also what it feels like to be child-like—to truly *experience* life in the moment and therefore be more carefree.

When we focus on what really matters, on what we and our children truly need, life becomes a whole lot simpler—and something as simple as a dirt pile suddenly becomes a whole lot of fun again. We can say joyfully with Paul, "And having food and clothing, with these we shall be content" (1 Timothy 6:8).

TRUE GODLINESS *with* CONTENTMENT
is itself GREAT WEALTH

—1 TIMOTHY 6:6 NLT

SOME QUESTIONS TO ASK YOURSELF:

• How much is enough?

• Where and what can you declutter from your life?

• Read Philippians 4:11–13 and consider how it does or does not reflect your life. Are you truly content? Or is your life full of striving?

Go Forward
by Going
Backward

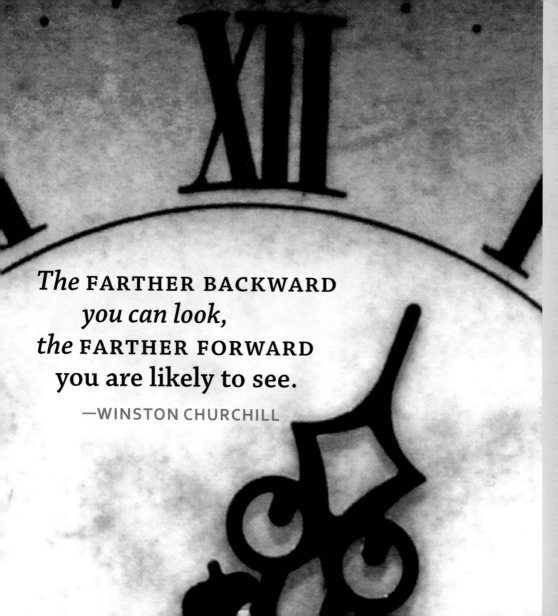

The FARTHER BACKWARD
you can look,
the FARTHER FORWARD
you are likely to see.

—WINSTON CHURCHILL

THERE ARE MANY BOOKS ON THE MARKET *that teach us how to "be in the present moment." Yet first we must learn to visit the future. How might our present lives take on new meaning if we think backward from what we envision for the future?*

The best way to plan ahead and reduce stress is to go backward.

When it comes to the future, there are **three kinds of people:** *those who let it happen,* **those who make it happen,** *and those who wonder what happened.*

—JOHN M. RICHARDSON JR.

That's right. I said, "Go forward by going backward." You see, to create a powerful life or supercharge your business, you have to experience your future *right now*. See it; feel it; be in it. Then go backward to the present.

I'm not proposing that we all pretend we're psychics or enlist their help to foretell our future. We don't need others to tell us our future. By faith we can take hold of the future God has for us. We can take stock in His plans for us, plans "of peace and not of evil, to give you a future and a hope" (Jeremiah 29:11). By trusting God for these plans right now, you can make an action plan for how to get there!

When I was a young child growing up in a very small town in rural Pennsylvania, I worked on the family farm as well as other farms and went to school in a one-room schoolhouse (believe it or not, one-room schoolhouses still existed when I was a kid). I walked to school each day, no matter what the weather, and when I got there, I had the opportunity to learn at my own pace. This open-classroom style allowed this young first grader to hear the teacher teaching second-grade and third-grade lessons as well. This environment helped me to develop a thirst for learning.

Although my family had very limited means and my mom sewed all of my clothes, I sat in that simple one-room schoolhouse and dreamed of a future in which I was a successful businessman, reading and learning from as many books as I ever wanted, and leading and motivating others.

Thanks to wonderful teachers and that one-room school-house's open-learning environment, I went on to graduate from college. My career path took me to various positions within the petroleum, marine, and outdoor recreational vehicle industries

Sit not down in despair;
hope on, hope ever.

—CHARLES SPURGEON

WE MUST TRUST GOD TODAY,

and leave the morrow

entirely with Him.

The present is ours;

the future belongs to God.

—E. M. BOUNDS

> Life must be UNDERSTOOD BACKWARDS.
> But . . . it must be LIVED FORWARDS.
>
> —SØREN KIERKEGAARD

and later to become president of a major U.S. division of a multi-national outdoor power equipment company.

Wherever you are in your life and career, you can take hold of God's promises, dream big, and take action in the present to make your dream happen.

The young boy named David who sat in that one-room school-house in homemade clothes is living proof that if you set your mind to your goals, you can acomplish them.

Go forward by going backward.

Some Questions to Ask Yourself:

- What future did you once dream for your life?

- Where are you now?

- If nothing can separate you from God's love and His plan for your life (Romans 8:38–39), then what are you afraid of?

- How can you trust God with your future more completely today?

Principle #5

Leave
the Past
Behind

I like the **DREAMS OF THE FUTURE** *better than the* **HISTORY OF THE PAST.**

—THOMAS JEFFERSON

WITHOUT REALIZING IT, *we often carry something around with us everywhere we go. We bring it out in our conversations, and it shows up in our attitudes. Whatever that thing is from the past may never have really existed, yet its power lives inside us and keeps us from moving forward.*

Listen to people talk throughout the day, and take note of where their conversations are grounded—in the future, in the present, or in the past. Where would you guess most conversations draw from?

The answer is the past.

"Forget about what's happened;
don't keep going over old history.
BE ALERT, BE PRESENT.
I'm about to do something brand-new."
—ISAIAH 43:18–19 MSG

Some of us take our past—and, therefore, stress—with us everywhere we go, towing it along behind us. Why do we do it? It's familiar to us. It's that warm and fuzzy bag of stories we like to take out and share with our family, friends, and coworkers. This comfortable past is often our "best friend." It's who and what we know best. It's like a worn-out easy chair or an old pair of shoes that fits us and feels just right. But God commands us, "Do not remember the former things, nor consider the things of old" (Isaiah 43:18), lest we miss the new thing He is doing right in front of us!

When people talk about or think about their past, it seems to take on the characteristics of a real-life being. The past cannot breathe, talk, think, or do. However, it is immensely powerful and can take over our future—if we let it. It's like the sirens on the shore,

Reflect upon your **present blessings,**
of which every man has many;
not on your **past misfortunes,**
of which all men have some.

—CHARLES DICKENS

luring you toward the rocks over and over again. Focusing on the past will certainly limit your choices for the future.

For a lot of people, I know the past holds a difficult childhood, an abusive marriage, or a financially draining job loss. Yet no matter how painful our past may have been, for some strange reason we often choose not to let go. In order to get on with our future and simplify our lives, we must choose to make a clean break.

There's an engaging *Peanuts* cartoon where Lucy is apologizing to Charlie Brown for missing a fly ball during a baseball game. She's sorry she missed the fly ball and says it's because she started remembering all the others she missed. "The past got in my eyes," she says.

Many of us know people who are very reasonable—they have very good reasons for why they can't move forward in life. Take for instance a person who has endured multiple bad relationships or marriages. He is certain that because of these relationships, he's stuck in the terrible spot he's in today. Isn't it difficult to watch that person once again become attracted to the same type of person with whom he just ended a contentious relationship?

Carrying the past forward to the future will provide us with only one thing—*incremental change*—in our lives. "Unreasonable" people make a choice to create *transformational breakthroughs,* without "reasonable" ties to the past.

Each of us has a powerful choice. We have the ability to create

I've got my *faults,*
but **living in the past** *is not one of them.*
There's *no future* in it.

—SPARKY ANDERSON,
MAJOR LEAGUE BASEBALL MANAGER

*We must always
obey the mandate—*
"ONWARD, ONWARD,
ONWARD."
—CHARLES SPURGEON

our own simplified future by starting with a blank sheet of paper and a heart surrendered to God's will for our lives.

Choose to leave your past behind, and begin living a life filled with new possibilities!

SOME QUESTIONS TO ASK YOURSELF:

- How has holding on to your past put limits on your future?

- What might you need to leave behind or let go of in order to move forward into the future?

- Is there a situation or a conversation from the past that you need to deal with in the present in order to move on to your future?

Principle #6

Choose to Be a Victor

The ONE THING
you can't take away from me
is the *way I choose to respond*
to what you do to me.
The LAST OF ONE'S FREEDOMS
is to choose one's attitude
in any given circumstance.

—VIKTOR FRANKL

ONE OF THE MOST POWERFUL MEDICINES *in the world is choice. We can choose our attitude, how we react to situations, and with whom we want to share our lives. When illnesses or situations threaten to disrupt our lives, it's our choice to throw in the towel and become a victim or stand and fight, no matter what the outcome—living the life we have as victors.*

A cheerful, confident **faith** is the ONLY SUCCESSFUL ATTITUDE *for* **the aspiring soul.**

—HANNAH WHITALL SMITH

No matter what your circumstances in life, you have a choice about your attitude toward them.

Whether it's the changing economy, difficult relationships, or a life-changing accident or illness, we possess the strongest mechanism there is to create a breakthrough: the power of attitude. We choose how we react, what we think about, and what we become—no matter what our surroundings or circumstances. We also choose how we want others to perceive us, acting and speaking accordingly.

In the fall of 2001, I awakened early one morning to get ready to spend the day at an industry trade show. While shaving, I noticed a lump on the side of my neck. It hadn't been there the day before. I was not feeling ill and, in fact, had just gotten a physical thirty days earlier and received a clean bill of health.

As soon as I got back into town a few days later, I called my family doctor. After explaining my situation, I got an appointment right away. My doctor took immediate action and sent me to a specialist. After a series of many tests, the diagnosis came back—lymphoma. That profoundly confrontational word—*cancer*—had just come to define my life.

It was a few weeks before the Christmas holidays, and the oncologist asked if I would like to wait to begin treatments until after the New Year. In my typical fashion of attacking a problem head-on, I said, "Let's get to work beating this thing *right now*." To be quite frank, I was scared to death. After living a very fast-paced life and conquering many challenges, nothing compares to the blatant nature of the *c*-word and the fact that your life may soon be over. Questions begin reeling through your mind: *Will I be here to see my grandchildren be born? Graduate? Get married?*

Attitude is
a little thing
that makes a
big difference.
—WINSTON CHURCHILL

ATTITUDES

determine our

ACTIONS,

for good or bad.

—D. L. MOODY

My treatment was set to begin with several months of chemo, followed by a month of radiation. Much to my surprise, while I was sitting in that chemo chair for the very first time, my best friend, Fred, walked into the room. He had come to be there with me. How do you quantify friendship like this?

During my treatment process, I encountered many folks with far worse diagnoses and much graver prognoses than my own. Life and all its intricacies was quickly put into proper perspective—so much so that when people would come into my office at work to tell me they had a problem, my first thought was, *No, you don't know what a real problem is.*

These folks I met in treatment became my heroes and offered me true inspiration. Their attitudes demonstrated they had chosen to live life victoriously, even if their life's duration might be a matter of

If you don't like something, *change it;*

if you can't change it, change the way you *think* about it.

—MARY ENGELBREIT

weeks or months. As a friend once told me, "Every day's a holiday and every meal's a picnic."

With early detection, the wisdom of great doctors, loving support from my family and friends, and overwhelming strength that can be found only in God in times like this, I was very fortunate to beat that cancer. I am pleased to report that I've been cancer-free ever since the end of those first chemo treatments.

When circumstances, people, or an illness threaten to get you down, remember that you *always* have a choice in how you react to and deal with the situation. Choose to confront challenges head-on, no matter how serious they are. And choose your friends wisely along the way. They'll be there for you when you need them, supporting and encouraging you to choose to lead a powerful life—one of a victor!

For the LORD YOUR GOD
is GOING WITH YOU!
He will FIGHT FOR YOU *against your enemies,*
and he will GIVE YOU VICTORY!

—DEUTERONOMY 20:4 NLT

SOME QUESTIONS TO ASK YOURSELF:

- What challenges are you facing today?

- Is your attitude a powerful match for them?

- Read Philippians 2. What was Jesus' attitude through all that He endured? How does your attitude compare to His?

Principle #7

Discover Your
Magnetism

If you have
  ZEST AND ENTHUSIASM,
you attract
  ZEST AND ENTHUSIASM.

Life does
  GIVE BACK IN KIND.
                    —NORMAN VINCENT PEALE

A MAGNET SERVES ITS PURPOSE *very well. It doesn't care exactly what it attracts. It's on auto-pilot and simply does its job. When we recognize that we too are magnets who attract people and things into our lives, we unleash the power to choose who and what we truly want to draw into our lives.*

Become wise by
WALKING WITH THE WISE;
hang out with fools
and watch your life **FALL TO PIECES.**

—PROVERBS 13:20 MSG

L ook around you. Who and what is in your life? Whoever and whatever you find, you've attracted. That's right. You brought them all to you. You're a magnet, and quite a powerful one at that.

Your thoughts, conversations, and actions have drawn everything and everyone to you just like a magnet attracts metal. Do you like what you see around you in your business, your job, or your personal life? Well, it's all because of you and God's grace in your life.

You didn't realize you had such a strong gravitational force, did you? Like it or not, you've pulled all these people and things into your pathway to the future. Do you want to keep them along for the ride?

If you're like me, you may have often heard your parents tell

The **best** mirror
is an **old friend.**

—GEORGE HERBERT

> A man who has friends
> must himself *be friendly.*
> —KING SOLOMON, PROVERBS 18:24

you when you were growing up something like, "You are who you have around you. Choose your friends and associates carefully." When I was a child, those words didn't have as much meaning and significance as they do today. Looking back on my life, I can see that I have been fortunate to have a number of people who positively influenced my life.

From the cancer victors to my friend Fred, to exceptional business associates like Rick, John, and George, to my executive coach Tony Smith—all helped me light up the scoreboard in business and friendship. I now know they didn't just happen to come into my life. My attitude, my conversations, and my way of being attracted them all to me.

Discover your magnetism, and choose carefully what you say, what you think, and what you do. Attract those people and things that will carry you forward to a desired state, one you choose to achieve—no matter what.

As iron
sharpens iron,
so a friend
sharpens a friend.

—PROVERBS 27:17 NLT

SOME QUESTIONS TO ASK YOURSELF:

- Who or what are you attracting in your life?

- As new people enter your life, how are they the same or different from others?

- Read Psalm 1. What kinds of influences from others should we avoid? What kinds should we seek out?

- Are your thoughts and conversations drawing powerful, positive influencers to you?

Principle #8

Get
Outdoors

GOD *writes the* **GOSPEL** *not in the* **BIBLE** *alone,*

but on **trees,** *and in the* **flowers** *and* **clouds** *and* **stars.**

—AUTHOR UNKNOWN

THE GREAT OUTDOORS PROVIDES MORE *than just beautiful scenery and a wealth of raw materials. Its true riches have been known for centuries. When we get outdoors, we can draw on these riches to guide us through whatever comes our way, just as God intends.*

Surely there is something in the **UNRUFFLED CALM OF NATURE** *that overawes our little anxieties and doubts; the sight of the* **deep-blue sky and the clustering stars above** *seems to impart a* **quiet to the mind.**

—JONATHAN EDWARDS

During the course of my career, I've had the pleasure of getting to know and learn from many wonderful people from all walks of life and backgrounds. A meeting I had with someone who was going to do a marketing project with my company opened my eyes to a fact I had never before come across. Yet having grown up on a farm, it had always been right before my eyes.

Tina Vindum is an outdoor fitness expert and author of *Tina Vindum's Outdoor Fitness*. She teaches exercise trainers, as well as her clients, to take their fitness regimens outdoors for improved results, both physically and mentally. When I met Tina for the first time, she shared what is referred to as the "biophilia effect." Scientists have discovered that, as human beings, we not only crave but have an innate need for the great outdoors. God's creation has a healing effect on us and serves as a natural stress reliever. It's no accident, then, that we fill our homes with plants and flowers or like to fall asleep listening to the sounds of a trickling brook or falling rain (whether real or generated by a sound machine).

Tina shared with me the results of a scientific study that showed that people in hospitals who had windows in their rooms often healed faster than those who didn't. In another study, scientists studied drivers with road rage and discovered that the smell of freshly cut grass decreased the blood pressure of stress-filled subjects.

The heavens *declare*
the GLORY OF GOD;
and the firmament shows
HIS HANDIWORK.

—KING DAVID, PSALM 19:1

Look deep into nature,
and then

you will **UNDERSTAND**
EVERYTHING **BETTER.**

—ALBERT EINSTEIN

In our challenging and often hectic world, nature provides us with an opportunity for healing and calming—take your cares outdoors, breathe deeply of the fresh air, walk among tall trees, and lift your eyes upward. You will quickly realize that no matter what obstacles you are facing, you and your worries are only a small part of the greater universe designed by our Creator. So get yourself outside and on the path to rejuvenation in body and spirit. And while you're out there, focus on the present. Listen for the birds singing. No matter what the weather, they are always rejoicing!

Look at that *beautiful* butterfly,
and learn from it to *trust in God*.

—JEREMY TAYLOR

SOME QUESTIONS TO ASK YOURSELF:

- How much time each day do you spend enjoying the outdoors?

- Read Psalm 19. While you are outside, are you made aware of God's glory in His creation?

- Do you have rooms with a view? Are you bringing nature inside your home or office (live plants, fountains, etc.) to create a serene environment?

Principle #9

Be Less
Iffy

But I focus on this
one thing:
FORGETTING THE PAST
and looking forward to
WHAT LIES AHEAD.
—PHILIPPIANS 3:13 NLT

LIFE IS LIVED HERE AND NOW. *Often we already have what we need, yet we look right past it hoping for something else to come our way.*

    If I only had more money . . .

    If I could own a house . . .

    If I only had a bigger house,

        a better job, a nicer car . . .

    If, if, if . . .

When one door closes, another opens;
but we often look so long and so regretfully
upon the closed door that we do not see
the one which has opened for us.

—ALEXANDER GRAHAM BELL

O ur wonderful country has afforded many of us exceptional opportunities to achieve and acquire many things. Yet we constantly hear stories of people who are extremely accomplished professionally and have vast riches or opportunities but are still incredibly unhappy. How can that be? A common misconception among humanity is that riches will bring happiness.

It's only a two-letter word, but that little word—*if*—stalls our growth and holds us back. When we "if" our lives away, we are giving away our power. We create a reason, an excuse, for why we aren't happy, fulfilled, and enriched by what we have today (and we have *so much* compared to most of the world). When King Solomon played this very game, he acquired everything under the sun and finally concluded that all of it "was all so meaningless—like chasing the wind" (Ecclesiastes 2:11 NLT). What could be less fulfilling than wind?

Countless individuals faithfully spend part of their paychecks each week trying to win the lottery. They're looking for that ticket that will provide for a totally carefree, happy life. Yet how many times do these big lottery winners appear in the local paper a year or two later saying how they lost their house, their spouse, and their friends and that their life was ruined by that "win"? "*If only* I hadn't won the lottery!"

When we have an iffy perspective on life, we choose to ride down a road filled with stop signs rather than enjoying our present. You are stopped and can't move forward when "if only" starts your day.

Choose to start living in the present, embracing a spirit of gratitude, and you will suddenly realize that the signs around you are all proclaiming, "Go!"

True contentment is a real,
even an active, virtue—not only
affirmative but creative.

It is the **power** of getting out
of any situation **all there is in it.**

—G. K. CHESTERTON

GOD, *you have made us* **FOR YOURSELF,** *and* **OUR HEARTS ARE RESTLESS** *till they find their* **REST IN YOU.**

—SAINT AUGUSTINE

SOME QUESTIONS TO ASK YOURSELF:

- Who and what are you most grateful for in your life?

- Read Ecclesiastes 5. If money can't buy fulfillment, where can it be found?

- What have you accomplished or what have you attained that you never imagined you'd have or achieve? Who can you thank for these things?

- Are you missing out on enjoying what's happening in the present by living with an "if only" mentality—wishing that something or someone else would come your way?

91

Principle #10

Make It a Purpose
to Know
Your
Purpose

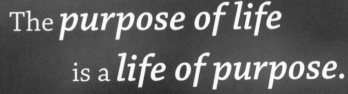

The *purpose of life* is a *life of purpose.*

—ROBERT BYRNE

BEFORE WE KNOW IT, *we are often flowing aimlessly down the river of life. We've left home without a map, and our boat has no rudder. What might that journey look like—and where might it ultimately lead—if we chose to live our lives with purpose?*

Great minds have PURPOSES; *others have* WISHES.

—WASHINGTON IRVING

My good friend and author Kevin McCarthy has written two books, *The On-Purpose Person* and *The On-Purpose Business*. Both have been key components of my business and personal life. In fact, I have given a copy of these books to every new vendor and employee I've met over the past ten years.

In *The On-Purpose Person*, Kevin artfully illustrates how each of us has a unique purpose in life. Our purpose is our heart and soul, a unique gift from God to each of us. Paul tells the Ephesians, "We are His workmanship, created in Christ Jesus for good works, which God prepared beforehand that we should walk in them" (2:10). It's who we are and why we exist. When we are "on-purpose," we are at our best, we are in the zone, we feel energized. We have meaning. When we are "off-purpose," we can become stressed.

The great use of a life is to spend it
for something that will **outlast** it.

—WILLIAM JAMES

The book tells the tale of a person in search of his purpose in life. He meets with a series of mentors who each give him a bit of help along the way to discovering his mission. It's a soulful book that makes us realize we each have the power to become a navigator rather than a drifter and to chart our course in life around our own true purpose.

Make it a goal to discover and live your purpose. Life will begin to take on new meaning and become something that touches, moves, and inspires not only you but also others around you.

Life without a purpose is a languid, drifting thing; every day we ought to **review our purpose,** saying to ourselves,

*"This day let me **make a sound beginning,** for what we have hitherto done is naught!"*

—THOMAS À KEMPIS

God has a purpose in **every life,** and when the ***soul is completely yielded*** and acquiescent,

   He will certainly realize it. Blessed is he who has never thwarted the ***working of the divine ideal.***

—F. B. MEYER

SOME QUESTIONS TO ASK YOURSELF:

- If you were designed for a reason, what do you think your unique role is?

- What are you truly passionate about? What lights you up?

- Consider some of the spiritual gifts Paul lists in Romans 12. Which ones has God given you? How can you put these gifts to work— at your job, within your family, in your local church fellowship?

- Do you have a mentor who helps guide you in your work or personal life?

Finally . . .

Slow Down to
Go Faster

*How sweet is
rest after fatigue!
How sweet will heaven be
when our journey is ended.*
—GEORGE WHITEFIELD

THERE'S A SAYING *in NASCAR that sometimes you have to slow down in order to go fast. In this complicated, fast-paced world of cell phones, the Internet, iPods, iPads, and smartphones, do you find it difficult to slow down? Sometimes life intervenes and does the "slowing" for us— whether it's an illness, a job loss, or the loss of a loved one. We often don't slow down by choice.*

Rest time is not waste time. . . .
It is wisdom to take occasional furlough.

In the long run, **we shall do more by sometimes doing less.**

—CHARLES SPURGEON

I f we never slow down, we might never take notice of the small and meaningful things that cross our paths; we might never fully recognize who and what are in our lives. By slowing down, we can take time to discover God's purpose for us and choose to fully live it each and every day.

Before something else intervenes on your behalf, choose to slow down. Take that vacation you've always dreamed about. Go back to school and learn a new trade or complete your degree. Downsize that big house to something you can actually afford. Read the job postings, and go for that new career or job you always wished for.

Making a move to the right-hand lane may make you think that life will pass you by. Yet choosing to slow down and simply trust in your Creator not only lets you enjoy the road along the way; it can supercharge you to reach your ultimate destination.

Life is designed by God to be enjoyed and lived fully. Allowing stress to take over is a choice that's completely in our control. Things happen in our lives, but choosing to respond with a Christlike attitude will make all the difference. Make a choice to stop being a stress magnet and instead attract a simplified way of being.

Talk to others who have simplified, and ask them how they

The LORD is good to those
who **wait for Him,**
to the soul
who **seeks Him.**

—LAMENTATIONS 3:25

SLOW DOWN
and everything you are chasing will
COME AROUND AND CATCH YOU.

—JOHN DE PAOLA

achieved it. Reduce the numbers, look for what's missing, and leave your past behind.

Ready to get out that blank sheet of paper? Whatever it is you want to attract or put into your life, begin with your thoughts. Proverbs 23:7 says, "For as he thinks in his heart, so is he." So what will you choose to dwell on? Who do you want to become? With whom will you choose to surround yourself? Find others who will support you and who are also committed to simplifying. What conversations do you need to have with them?

Once you start the process of slowing down in order to win the race, you will discover that stress is indeed a choice—and a choice you don't need to make. Less stress is yours for the taking.

Half our life is spent **TRYING TO FIND SOMETHING** *TO DO* **with the time we have RUSHED THROUGH LIFE** *TRYING TO SAVE.*

—WILL ROGERS

May the LORD SMILE ON YOU
and BE GRACIOUS TO YOU.

May the LORD SHOW YOU HIS FAVOR
and GIVE YOU PEACE.

—NUMBERS 6:25–26 NLT

ABOUT *the Author*

A leader with an innate talent to touch, move, and inspire others, David Zerfoss lives his purpose of "empowering others to create powerful futures." An accomplished business professional who is highly skilled in transformational leadership, executive coaching, and public speaking, Zerfoss connects with people from all walks of life. He draws on personal life examples, from growing up on a farm in rural Pennsylvania, where he attended a one-room schoolhouse, to achieving hundreds of millions of dollars in sales increases during his eighteen-year tenure as president of Husqvarna Professional Products, Inc.

Dave is a down-to-earth individual who believes in big ideas and bold declarations. He leads the Zerfoss Group, which consults with think tanks, major corporations, and entrepreneurs. As an executive-in-residence at Queens University McColl School of Business in Charlotte, North Carolina, he enjoys sharing transformational thinking and leadership insights with aspiring MBA and executive MBA students. He resides in Davidson, North Carolina, with his wife, Barbara.